D1061336

IMAGES *of* IRELAND

CHRONICLE BOOKS

SAN FRANCISCO

Out-worn heart, in a time out-worn,
　　Come clear of the nets of wrong and right;
Laugh, heart, again in the grey twilight,
Sigh, heart, again in the dew of the morn.

Your mother Eire is always young,
Dew ever shining and twilight grey;
Though hope fall from you and love decay,
Burning in fires of a slanderous tongue.

Come, heart, where hill is heaped upon hill:
For there the mystical brotherhood
Of sun and moon and hollow and wood
And river and stream work out their will;

And God stands winding His lonely horn,
And time and the world are ever in flight;
And love is less kind than the grey twilight,
And hope is less dear than the dew of the morn.

W. B. YEATS, *INTO THE TWILIGHT*

UPPER LAKE, GLENDALOUGH, CO WICKLOW

Still south I went and west and south again,
  Through Wicklow from the morning till the night,
And far from cities, and the sights of men,
Lived with the sunshine, and the moon's delight.

I knew the stars, the flowers, and the birds,
The grey and wintry sides of many glens,
And did but half remember human words,
In converse with the mountains, moors, and fens.

JOHN MILLINGTON SYNGE, *PRELUDE*

LANDSCAPE, CO DONEGAL

There is perpetual kindness in the Irish cabin – butter-milk, potatoes – a stool is offered or a stone is rolled that your honour may sit down and be out of the smoke, and those who beg everywhere else seem desirous to exercise free hospitality in their own houses. Their natural disposition is turned to gaiety and happiness: while a Scotsman is thinking about the term-day, or if easy on that subject, about hell in the next world – while an Englishman is making a little hell in the present, because his muffin is not well roasted – Pat's mind is always turned to fun and ridicule.

SIR WALTER SCOTT, *DIARY*

COTTAGE, ASKEATON, CO LIMERICK

Who were the builders? Question not the silence
     That settles on the lake for evermore,
Save where the sea-bird screams and to the islands
The echo answers from the steep-cliffed shore.
O half-remaining ruin, in the lore
Of human life a gap shall all deplore
Beholding thee; since thou art like the dead
Found slain, no token to reveal the why,
The name, the story. Some one murdered
We know, we guess; and gazing upon thee,
And, filled by the long silence of reply,
We guess some garnered sheaf of tragedy; –
Of tribe or nation slain so utterly
That even their ghosts are dead, and on their grave
Springeth no bloom of legend in its wildness;
And age by age weak washing round the islands
No faintest sigh of story lisps the wave.

WILLIAM LARMINIE, *THE NAMELESS DOON*

DUNGUAIRE CASTLE, KINVARA, CO GALWAY

Snow was general all over Ireland. It was falling on every part of the dark central plain, on the treeless hills, falling softly upon the Bog of Allen and, farther westward, softly falling into the dark mutinous Shannon waves. It was falling too, upon every part of the lonely churchyard on the hill where Michael Furey lay buried. It lay thickly drifted on the crooked crosses and headstones, on the spears of the little gate, on the barren thorns. His soul swooned slowly as he heard the snow falling faintly through the universe and faintly falling, like the descent of their last end, upon all the living and the dead.

JAMES JOYCE, *THE DEAD*

SNOW SCENE, CO WICKLOW

I walked through Ballinderry in the springtime,
When the bud was on the tree,
And I said, in every fresh-ploughed field beholding
The sowers striding free,
Scattering broadcast, for the corn in golden plenty,
On the quick, seed-clasping soil,
Even such this day among the fresh-stirred hearts of Erin
Thomas Davis, is thy toil!

SAMUEL FERGUSON, *LAMENT FOR THE DEATH OF THOMAS DAVIS*

Dublin in the early morning, with the sun shining, is a city the colour of claret. The red-brick Georgian mansions, with fine doors, fanlights, and little iron balconies at the first-floor windows, stand back in well-bred reticence against wide roads, quiet and dignified, as if the family had just left by stage-coach. Dublin shares with Edinburgh the air of having been a great capital.

This city is as completely a creation of the eighteenth century as Bath. It is a superb, indolent aristocrat among cities, with an easy manner and a fine air of unstudied elegance. The Liffey, crossed by eight bridges, some of them good-looking, cuts the city into a north and south division, and there is pervading Dublin that subtle something as vivid and distinctive as the feel of ships and docks, due to the nearness of great mountains. Just behind Dublin the long, smooth Wicklow Hills lie piled, clear-cut against the sky, brown-green in colour, and from them on clear days, I am told, a man can see across the Irish Sea to the mountains of Wales.

H.V. MORTON, *IN SEARCH OF IRELAND*

GEORGIAN DOORS, DUBLIN

Ne thence the Irishe Rivers absent were,
  Sith no lesse famous then the rest they bee,
And joyne in neighbourhood of kingdom nere,
Why should they not likewise in love agree,
And joy likewise this solemne day to see?
They saw it all, and present were in place;
Though I them all according their degree,
Cannot recount, nor tell their hidden race,
Nor read the savage countries, through which they place.

EDMUND SPENSER, *THE FAERIE QUEENE*

Close at our feet was a grass field full of yellow ragweed and a hedge overgrown with loosestrife springing among a creamy froth of meadow-sweet. Everything was a part of an unstudied pageant. Man seems very small in those wide, spacious, and wind-swept regions; the moving waters have little to do in their priest-like task of pure ablution, for earth's shores have little soil of humanity. Yet everywhere the mountain-sides show here and there a patch of tillage, some field of corn nestled into a nook of the hills, here and there a rough-built cottage whose thatch and walls are weathered into soft greys and browns, and the presence of these features, rather felt than noticed, gives to the whole land-scape the kindly human touch.

STEPHEN GWYNN, *THE CHARM OF IRELAND*

FARM COTTAGE, CO CAVAN

Oh, where, Kincora! is Brian the Great?
And where the beauty that once was thine?
Oh, where are the princes and nobles that sate
At the feast in thy halls, and drank the red wine?
Where, oh Kincora?

....

They are gone, those heroes of royal birth,
Who plundered no churches, and broke no trust,
'Tis weary for me to be living on earth
While they, oh, Kincora, lie low in the dust!
Low, oh Kincora!

ATTRIBUTED TO MAC LIAG (TRANS. JAMES CLARENCE MANGAN), *KINCORA*

ROUND TOWER AND CRANNOG NEAR OMAGH, CO TYRONE

I was at first surprised at the apparently abstemious habits of the Irish gentry. To take only a half glass of whisky and cold water seemed to be the excess of moderation. But I quickly discovered that the half glass was merely the thin side of the wedge, and only a prelude to a night's jollification....

After about two hours thus spent, and when the party are thoroughly hilarious and uproarious, though rarely drunk, or, to use a more refined expression, intoxicated, there is a pause in the conversation, and a discussion ensues as to the propriety of going home. This proposition is generally carried, that is so far as the second reading or principle is concerned. Then a further discussion ensues as to what they shall have before going home, and after various liquors being considered the almost invariable conclusion arrived at is the favourite order for another half glass of whisky, which is repeated two or three times, and then the party breaks up, and the surprise is that they can assume a standing position at all, but somehow or other a party of Irish gentlemen will generally contrive to leave an inn in good order and so as to avoid anything like scandal.

W.W. BARRY, *A WALKING TOUR ROUND IRELAND*

DANIEL W. BOLLARD'S PUB, KILKENNY

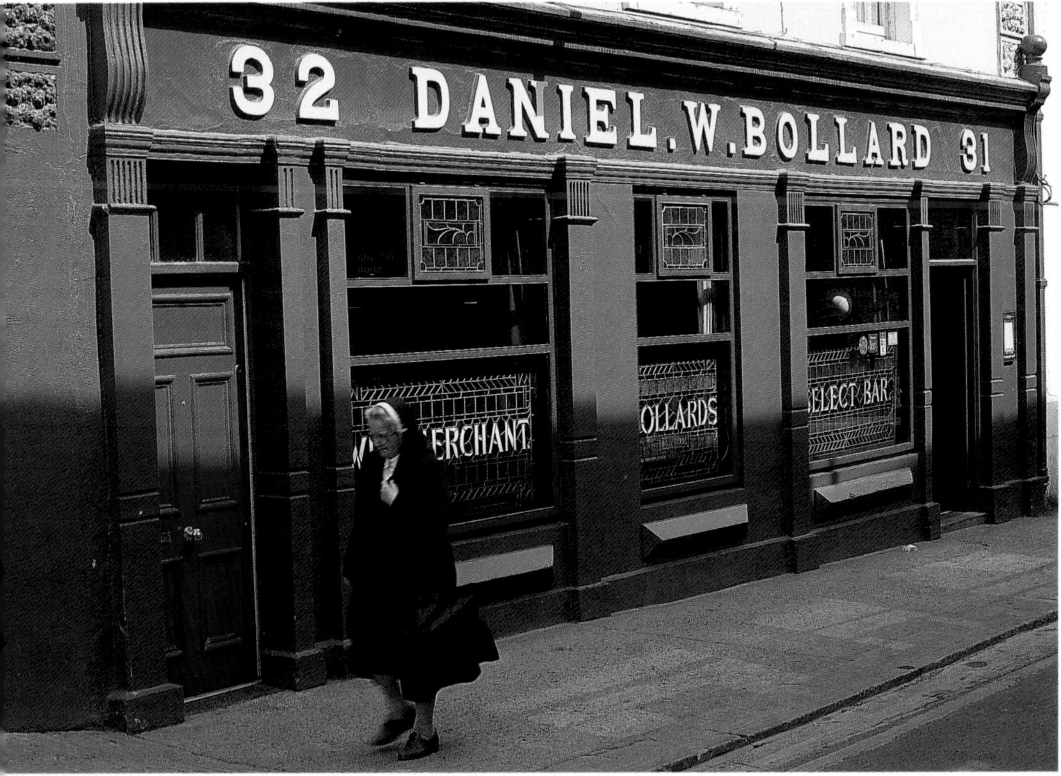
32 DANIEL. W. BOLLARD 31

We are the music-makers
And we are the dreamers of dreams,
Wandering by lone sea-breakers,
And sitting by desolate streams; –
World-losers and world-forsakers,
On whom the pale moon gleams:
Yet we are the movers and shakers
Of the world for ever, it seems.

With wonderful deathless ditties
We build up the world's great cities,
And out of a fabulous story
We fashion an empire's glory:
One man with a dream, at pleasure,
Shall go forth and conquer a crown;
And three with a new song's measure
Can trample an empire down.

ARTHUR O'SHAUGHNESSY, *ODE*

IRISH MUSICIANS

To Aran assuredly should go any visitor of Galway who does not fear thirty miles of sea. The Dun Angus steamer plies regularly back and forward.

I have seen nothing stranger than these rocks where nearly all the ground surface is covered by great slabs of limestone, rising tier by tier till at last the western face towers up a thousand feet. Islanders all use the *pampootie*, or slipper of raw hide, held together with thongs, for walking on these slippery surfaces; just as instead of ordinary rowing-boats they use *curraghs* or canoes of wickerwork covered with tarred canvas, which ride on top of the water and go climbing up the slope of an Atlantic wave like a vast water-beetle. I doubt if anywhere else in these islands is there a way of life so remote and strange to the city-dweller. Yet many of these people can talk familiarly of Boston and Philadelphia.

STEPHEN GWYNN, *THE CHARM OF IRELAND*

STORM AT INISMORE, ARAN ISLANDS

The dolmen was in a thicket, a few fields from the road. It was composed of the usual three great vertical slabs of stone with a capstone over them. Once they had been covered by a cairn, but the stones had recently been carted away for wall-building, and only this central chamber remained, with its ring of standing stones to mark the original boundary of the cairn. This was a good instance of a so-called 'Druid's' altar that, obviously, had never been more than a tomb. All over the country we find these megalithic remains, and again and again they are ascribed to the Druids. In actual fact they were in existence at least a thousand years before the Druids appeared in Ireland, about the fifth century BC. It is, of course, possible that the Druids, finding these imposing structures already in being, made use of them for their own rites and ceremonies, much as Christians have converted many pagan memorials to their uses.

ROBERT GIBBINGS, *LOVELY IS THE LEE*

DOLMEN, POULNABRONE, CO CLARE

We did not think it possible to see the lake in any new aspect, yet there it lay as we had never seen it before, so still, so soft, so grey, like a white muslin scarf flowing out, winding past island and headland. The silence was so intense that one thought of the fairy books of long ago, of sleeping woods and haunted castles; there were the castles on islands lying in misted water, faint as dreams. Now and then a bird uttered a piercing little chatter from the branches of the tall larches, and ducks talked in the reeds, but their talk was only a soft murmur, hardly louder than the rustle of the reeds now in full leaf. Everything was spellbound that day; the shadows of reed and island seemed fixed for ever as in a magic mirror – a mirror that somebody had breathed upon, and, listening to the little gurgle of the water about the limestone shingle, one seemed to hear eternity murmuring its sad monotony.

GEORGE MOORE, *MEMOIRS OF MY DEAD LIFE*

First published in the United States in 1994
by Chronicle Books

Design Copyright © 1994 by Russell Ash & Bernard Higton

ISBN 0-8118-0614-6

Chronicle Books
275 Fifth Street
San Francisco, California
94103

1 2 3 4 5 6 7 8 9 10

Photographs: Cover, pages 11, 19, 21, 23: The Slide File;
3, 5, 7, 9, 13, 27, 29, 31: Images Colour Library;
15: Comstock Photo Library;
17: Adam Woolfitt/Robert Harding Picture Library;
25: Walter Pfeiffer Studios.